DEALING WITH...
FAMILY CHANGES
Mitchell Lane
PUBLISHERS
KELLI HICKS

Parent and Caregiver Tips for Creating Nonfiction Readers

Timely topics in the *Dealing With...* series will interest intermediate and middle school readers and equip them with helpful strategies for coping with difficult situations. Your reader will be introduced to new concepts, facts, ideas, and vocabulary.

Tips for Reading Nonfiction

Talk about Nonfiction

Explain that nonfiction books provide facts about real-world topics. When readers read nonfiction, they gain a rich understanding of the world. They build background knowledge that provides a foundation for learning and academic success.

Look at the Parts

This book contains the following helpful features. Share the purpose of each feature with your reader.

Photos, Captions, and Graphic Aids
The photos, captions, charts, and other graphic aids in nonfiction texts contain a wealth of information. Help your reader identify different ways information can be displayed.

Sidebars
These extra tidbits of information help satisfy readers' curiosity and expand their knowledge.

Table of Contents
Located at the front of the book, this list shows the big ideas within the text and the page numbers where they can be found.

Extension Activities and Additional Resources
A "Your Turn" quiz and "Exploration and Discovery" activities invite readers to apply their new knowledge. Supporting resources are provided in a special "You Are Not Alone" section.

Glossary
Located at the back of the book, the glossary defines key words and phrases that are related to the topic. These words and phrases can be found in the text in **bold** type.

Index
Located at the back of the book, the index is an alphabetical list of topics and the page numbers where they can be found.

With a little help and guidance, your reader will be on their way to enjoying and learning from nonfiction books.

Mitchell Lane
PUBLISHERS
mitchelllanepub.com

2001 SW 31st Avenue
Hallandale, FL 33009

First Edition, 2026.
Author: Kelli Hicks
Designer: Rhea Magaro
Editor: Kim Thompson

Series: Dealing With...
Title: Dealing with Family Changes / by Kelli Hicks

Hallandale, FL : Mitchell Lane Publishers, [2026]

Library bound ISBN: 979-8-89260-673-8
eBook ISBN: 979-8-89260-680-6

PHOTO CREDITS
Shutterstock: Ground Picture, cover, 1; PeopleImages.com - Yuri A, 5, 7, 14, 36, 41; stockfour, 6; Phairoh chimmi, 8; Face Stock, 9; Krakenimages.com, 10, 37; goir, 12; AJR_photo, 13; Antonio Guillem, 15; fizkes, 16; Africa Studio, 17; Zurijeta, 18; Black Salmon, 19; africa_pink, 20; ESB Professional, 21; Cookie Studio, 22; Lapina, 23; Stock 4you, 24; Lopolo, 25, 33, 47; abstract.rita, 26; Kamira, 27; Monkey Business Images, 28; Ribkhan, 29; Lokana, 30; Manuela Durson, 32; Red Fox studio, 33; Inside Creative House, 34; JOURNEY STUDIO7, 35; Perfect Wave, 38; Fellers Photography, 39; iofoto, 42; Pixel-Shot, 44

Table of Contents

Chapter 1: Safe and Happy

Harper

Harper bounced into her room. She plunked down at her desk and started her homework, but she couldn't stop grinning. She just found out that she earned a spot on her community's top soccer team. It was a dream come true!

Harper's smile grew as she remembered the best news of all. Her two friends also made the team. The three had been best friends since kindergarten. They often hung out together and had weekend sleepovers. Now, they would play soccer together too!

Harper thought about all the good things to come. She imagined winning games with her new team. She imagined spending lots of time with her best friends through middle school and beyond. Harper's world felt safe and full of routines that made her happy.

Just then, Harper's mom appeared at the door. Her face looked sad and a little worried. Harper could tell something was really wrong. Beads of sweat broke out on Harper's forehead.

"I have some news," Harper's mom said. "Grandma had a bad fall. She's okay, but she needs surgery. Then, she'll need lots of care. She can't live alone anymore. We'll move in with her. Her house has plenty of room."

Tears sprang to Harper's eyes. She felt awful for her grandma. But she also felt bad for herself. This wasn't part of Harper's plan! "For how long?" she asked shakily.

Harper's mom tried to sound excited. "For a while," she said. "Maybe permanently. We'll look into transferring you to the new school. It's a great town. I know you'll like it there."

Harper was **devastated**. She felt her whole world turn upside down. How was she ever going to be okay?

What Do You Think?

- How does Harper feel at different points in the story? Why?
- How is Harper's relationship with her friends different than her relationship with her family members?
- How do you react to changes? Do they make you excited or fearful?
- Has your family experienced changes? How have they affected you?

Chapter 2: What Are Family Changes?

Life is full of change. There are small changes like getting a new hairstyle, trying a new food, or learning how to solve a new type of math problem. There are bigger changes like owning a new pet, going to a new school, or getting braces on your teeth.

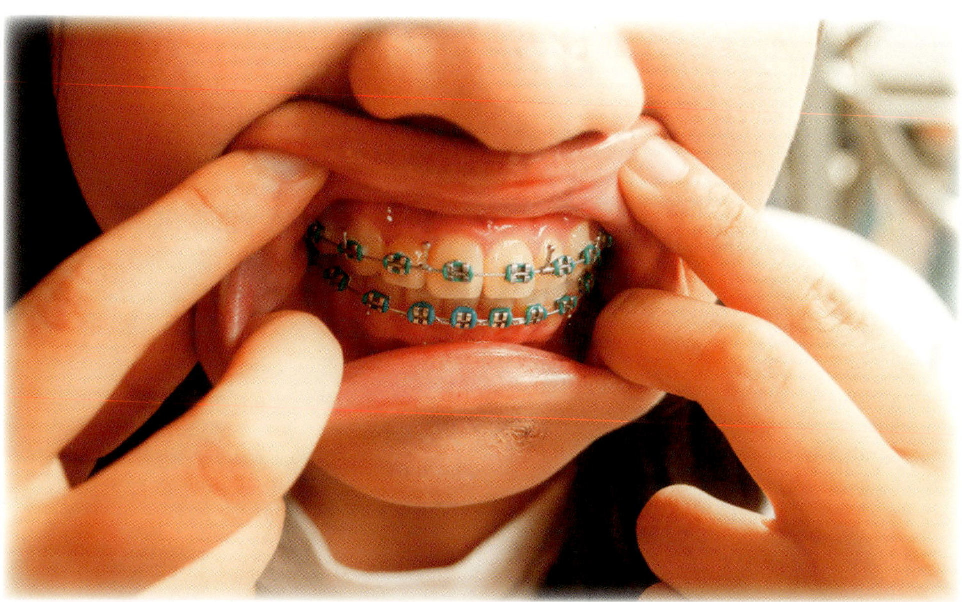

Did You Know?

Most people experience major changes in their lives, or "lifequakes," every 12 to 18 months.

Some people like change because it brings new and surprising events. They get excited when they don't know what will happen next. Other people **resist** change. They want things to feel familiar and safe. They are most comfortable with **predictable** routines.

Change can be good. But if you are like most people, even small changes can make you a bit nervous. New situations and challenges might cause your heart to beat a little faster or make you feel like you have butterflies in your stomach. Big changes affect you in bigger ways. Major **disruptions** to your life can be downright scary.

Your family members have known you since you were a baby. They have helped you and cared for you your whole life. They are part of the **foundation** of your world. That's why family changes can be especially hard to **cope** with. When things in your family change, it is easy to feel unsettled or **overwhelmed**.

Types of Family Changes

All families change. Babies are born. Older people reach the end of their lives. Couples get together or break up. Families grow, shrink, move, face challenges, and **adapt** in many different ways.

Any changes to your family have a big impact on your life. That's because they involve the people you are closest to. Here are some common family changes that can seem to turn your life upside down.

- Birth of a brother, sister, cousin, or other family member
- Addition of a live-in family member, such as a stepbrother, stepsister, or relative
- Getting a new stepparent
- Illness or injury of a family member
- Death of a grandparent or other family member
- Divorce or separation
- Moving to a new place
- A parent or other family member losing a job
- A parent or other family member starting a new job
- Financial problems
- Having very busy schedules
- Fighting among family members

Studies Show That...
About 50 years ago, 67 percent of American families were made up of married parents and their children living in the same home. Since then, that number has gone down to only 37 percent of families.

Family Changes and the Brain

Family changes can bring feelings of **stress**. When you encounter stress, a part of your brain called the amygdala jumps into action. The amygdala is like a guard, always on the lookout for danger. If it senses a problem, it can make you feel scared or angry. It floods your body with **adrenaline** and **cortisol**.

Adrenaline and cortisol work together to tell your brain and body to get ready for action. They help you react quickly, without having to think too much. This stress response is known as "fight-or-flight" because it can help you escape danger or defend yourself, if needed.

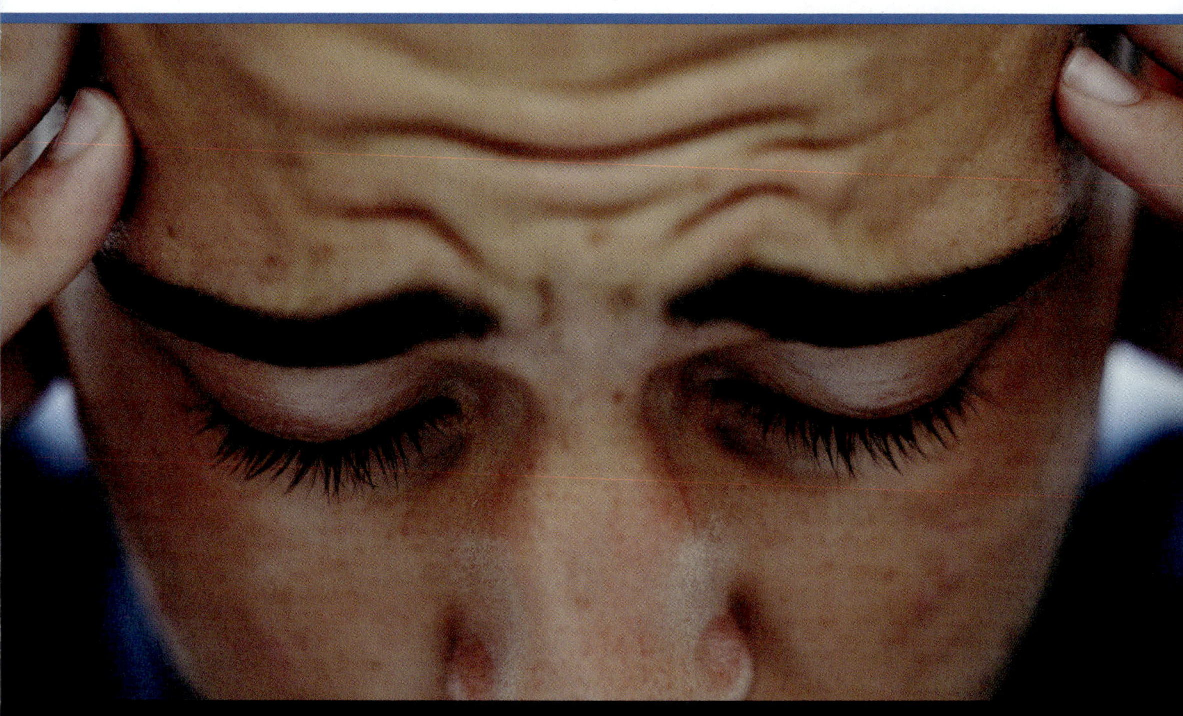

Studies Show That...

Young people who experience severe stress may have reduced activity in a part of the brain called the hippocampus. This can lead to problems with learning and memory.

But here's the thing: Fear and anger aren't always the best responses to stress. Many challenges require clear thinking and thoughtful actions. When adrenaline and cortisol are released, it can be hard to think deeply or to feel complex emotions.

Over time, stress impacts your health. It makes you feel tired and unfocused. It causes stomachaches, headaches, and sore muscles. It can lead to serious mental health challenges like **anxiety** and **depression**.

With practice, you can improve your brain's ability to handle stress. People who are **resilient** bounce back quickly after upsetting experiences. They easily adapt and adjust to change. When others feel hopeless, they feel ready to try something new.

The secret to becoming more resilient is understanding that your brain has neuroplasticity. That means it reorganizes itself as you have new experiences and think about things in new ways.

When change happens in your family, you can decide to take positive actions. You can choose to see the change as an opportunity instead of a threat. Over time, your brain will start to think this way all the time. You will become more **optimistic** in the face of change.

There IS Good News!

Resilient people are able to recognize and name their feelings. They believe that they are in the driver's seat of their own lives. They understand that their actions and attitude can make a positive difference.

Family Changes and Individual Differences

Different people respond to change in different ways. For some people, it is easy to go with the flow and adjust to new situations. Other people find it more difficult to adapt. Some changes, like a death in the family, are so big that they challenge even the most resilient people.

Did You Know?

Family changes can be especially hard for people who have ADHD, autism, or anxiety. These people tend to do best when things are predictable and structured. Changes that disrupt their usual routines can cause stress and confusion.

No matter how you react to change, it is important to accept your feelings. Be kind to yourself. Remember that circumstances just happen. They are not your fault, and they don't mean that anything is wrong with you. Changes don't affect your ability to be happy and to make decisions about your own life.

Chapter 3: Signs of Family Changes

Dealing with family changes is hard. It can affect all parts of your life. When you are worried about your family, it is difficult to sleep well and eat healthy meals. It can be challenging to concentrate on schoolwork. You may not have the time or energy to do normal activities and spend time with your friends.

Did You Know?

Physical problems can be seen. If you break your arm, you get a cast. If you have a cold, you sneeze. But emotional stress is not always visible. It can be hard for others to know how you are feeling. It is important to express your emotions and ask for help.

It is common to experience shifting emotions. It may feel like you are on a roller coaster, with many ups and downs. You might be convinced that everything is going wrong in one moment but feel happy in the next. This is all normal.

The Stages of Change

Dealing with family changes takes time and effort. It is a process. Researchers have found that most people go through four stages as they face change and make adjustments in their lives.

Stage 1: Shock

When people first learn about a big change in their families, they feel **disoriented**. They are confused and uncertain. They experience a sense of **shock**. It is okay to be in this stage. Your brain and body need time to confront the news and understand what has happened. Focus on staying calm and taking care of yourself.

Stage 2: Anger

In this stage, strong emotions often take over. You did not ask for this change to your family. It was not in your plans. It feels unfair. It feels scary. It makes you angry. It is okay to be in this stage for a while. You are allowed to feel the way you do. But do not take your feelings out on yourself or others. Acknowledge your emotions, but do not let them control your actions.

Stage 3: Acceptance

In this stage, you begin to see some positive sides to your changed family. You may enjoy spending time with a new family member. You may notice things to like about a new home or new school. You may find new roles in your family that make you happy. You start to accept the change and come to terms with it.

Stage 4: Commitment

The last stage is committing to your changed life. You want to work toward new goals. After your grandfather dies, you may decide to honor him by telling jokes like he used to do. After your parents get divorced, you may commit to making new friends in two different neighborhoods. You feel strong and ready to face the future.

When Are Family Changes a Problem?

Sometimes, a family change is more than you can handle on your own. You may not progress through the stages of adjusting to change. You might get stuck feeling shocked or angry. Constant stress may lead to mental health problems like anxiety or depression.

Feelings of extreme stress and sadness can change your health and your behavior. You may experience physical symptoms like headaches or stomachaches. You may act out and get into trouble at home or at school. You may **isolate** yourself from friends and family members. These are all problems. They are warning signs that you need help adjusting to a family change. Talk to a trusted adult right away.

Chapter 4: Strategies for Taking Control

Dealing with changes in your family can be difficult, but don't worry! There are many strategies you can use to make things easier and help you feel more in control.

Strategy #1: Express Your Feelings

Keeping your emotions bottled up inside doesn't make them go away. Expressing your feelings is healthy and necessary. It helps you let off steam and better understand yourself. It helps others understand what you are going through and what you need. Follow these steps.

1. Notice your feelings and their effects. Are they making you lonely? Sick? Restless? Tune in to your body and what it is telling you.

2. Name your feelings. Say them out loud or write them down. Are you frustrated? Sad? Worried? Angry? Naming your emotions takes away some of their power over you.

3. Accept and **validate** your feelings. It is normal to feel the way you do. It is understandable. It is okay.

4. Let your feelings out. Share them with people you trust. Be honest. Use "I" statements such as "I feel afraid" or "I feel like I have lost something important to me."

Strategy #2: Follow Routines

No matter what is going on with your family, creating routines can help you manage your time and reduce stress. Think about what you need and want to do each day. Set a schedule and follow it. Include time for sleep, school, exercise, homework, chores, and being with friends.

Try to stick to your schedule even if other things get in the way. Let family members know that you need time to take care of yourself. Explain that your routines help you feel calm and organized.

TUESDAY
WEDNESDAY
THURSDAY
FRIDAY
SATURDAY
SUNDAY
LASSON
TIME
1
2
3
4
5
History
Drawing
Spanish
Spanish
LUNCH
Public Speaking
Advisory
Calculus
Chemistry
History
LUNCH
English
History
Drawing
Calculus
Spanish
LUNCH
English
Public Speaking
Advisory
Chemistry
Calculus
English
Literature
LUNCH
English
English
Literature
LUNCH
English
Basketball
Swimming
Art
Basketball
Swimming
Art
Art
Astronomy

Strategy #3: Practice Healthy Habits

Having healthy habits helps you deal with stress and adapt to changes. Eating a balance of protein, fruits, vegetables, and whole grains helps your body function at its best. Avoid foods that are high in sugar or that are highly processed. Cookies may taste good, but they will not provide the fuel you need to face the day.

There Is Good News!

Want a boost for your brain and your mood? Go outside! Spending time in nature makes you feel happier and more relaxed. It's like a reset button for your thoughts and feelings.

Try to keep a regular sleep schedule. Go to bed at the same time each night and wake up at the same time each day. Plan to sleep for at least eight hours at night. If you need a nap during the day, limit it to 20 minutes so that it won't disrupt your nightly sleep schedule.

Staying active keeps you physically and mentally healthy. It is also a great way to relieve stress and spend time with friends. When you exercise, your brain releases hormones called endorphins that make you feel good.

Strategy #4: Stay Connected

When you are dealing with lots of change, you might just want to be alone. But isolating yourself from others actually makes things worse. Research shows that staying connected to family and friends reduces stress and helps you feel safe.

Choose to be around positive people who make you feel good about yourself. Having people in your life who listen to you and support you improves your mental health. Take time to chat, do things together, or just hang out. This strategy is especially helpful when you are spending time away from one parent or old friends.

Did You Know?

Spending time on social media is not a good strategy for dealing with stress. It can make you feel lonelier. It can make you compare yourself to others and think you're the only one who has problems. That just isn't true.

Strategy #5: Make Your Own Choices

When changes happen in your family, you may feel like you can't choose where you are or what you are doing. At different times, you may be required to live with one parent or the other. You may have to support family members instead of doing your own activities. Situations like these aren't your fault, but they can feel limiting.

Remind yourself that you always have choices. There are always chances to learn, grow, and be happy. Will you live at your dad's new apartment during a school break? Ask him if there is room to set up an area for a craft or hobby you want to try. Do you have to go to your sister's volleyball tournament? Take along a game you like and find other kids who want to play.

Strategy #6: Practice Gratitude

Even in the middle of big changes, there are things to be thankful for. Practicing gratitude means appreciating the good things in your life. It turns your attention toward things that bring you joy and make you proud of yourself. It helps you focus on the positive and recognize what is going well.

Studies Show That...

Showing gratitude has positive effects on your mind and body. It can improve your sleep quality, reduce your anxiety, and help you manage your emotions.

Use a notebook or an app to keep a gratitude journal. Write about things you are grateful for and explain why. For example, you might write *I am grateful for my bicycle because I feel great when I ride it* or *I am grateful for my dog because her kisses make me smile.*

Chapter 5: Dealing with Family Changes

Remember Harper? For days, she was in shock about her family's move. She felt numb. Then, one day after her grandma came home from the hospital, Harper was sitting in her grandma's kitchen. She began to sob. Her mom and grandma came right away. Harper couldn't keep her feelings in. She told them she felt sad and scared. She expressed anger about leaving her old life behind. The women listened. They hugged Harper and told her they understood.

Little by little, Harper adjusted. She loved spending time with her grandma. She explored the attic and found some cool items for her new room. She even met some nice neighbor kids. Harper made a plan to learn about soccer teams in her new town. She was keeping a list of places to take her best friends when they came to visit.

Moving had been hard, but it brought new possibilities. Harper's family had changed, but she still had a bright future and many reasons to feel grateful and happy.

Remember: Family changes are difficult, but they get easier with time. You have the power to be resilient and to view changes as opportunities for growth and happiness.

YOUR TURN: HOW DO YOU DEAL WITH FAMILY CHANGES?

For each situation, select the answer most likely to produce the best outcome. Make a note of your answers on a separate sheet of paper.

1. Jackson has had his own bedroom since he was little. Now, he has to share his room with his stepbrother. What can he do to feel less angry about it?
   - **A.** Keep the light on all night so his stepbrother has a hard time sleeping.
   - **B.** Acknowledge his angry feelings and express them to a friend.
   - **C.** Skip dinner so he can have some time alone in his room.

2. Samira's birthday falls on a weekend when she will be with her dad. But she wants to celebrate with friends who live closer to her mom. What can she do?
   - **A.** Ask her dad about meeting her friends halfway at an ice cream shop.
   - **B.** Keep quiet. What she wants doesn't matter anyway.
   - **C.** Settle for celebrating her birthday on a different day.

3. Zac's new baby cousin is at his house all the time. It bothers him when she cries and distracts him from his homework. What should Zac do?
   - **A.** Ignore his homework and watch TV instead.
   - **B.** Stay alone in his room and wear headphones.
   - **C.** Ask if he can play with the baby before doing his homework. Maybe he can make her smile.

4. Kaitlin's aunt is getting treatment for breast cancer. Kaitlin can't stop worrying about her. What should she do?
   - **A.** Call her aunt to chat, then go outside to take a bike ride.
   - **B.** Do nothing and let her stress and anxiety build up.
   - **C.** Ignore her aunt so she doesn't have to deal with her feelings.

Think about your answers.

1. The best answer is B. Acknowledging his emotions, naming them, and talking to a friend will help Jackson manage his stress and adapt to the change.
2. The best answer is A. Samira deserves to make choices that matter to her. She can talk to her dad to find a creative solution for having a happy birthday.
3. The best answer is C. Zac can choose to view time with his new cousin as an opportunity to bond with her while following his usual routines.
4. The best answer is A. Kaitlin can support her aunt while still following her own routines and managing her stress. Exercise and fresh air will improve her outlook.

EXPLORATION AND DISCOVERY: ACTIVITIES TO TRY

1. Think about three events or changes in your family that have felt unfair to you. Then, think of a way to be optimistic about each situation and reframe it as an opportunity.
2. Create a new routine that will improve your physical or mental health. It could be eating a healthy snack at the same time each day, learning to play a new sport, or meeting a friend for a walk. Practice the routine until it becomes a habit.
3. Try breathing exercises when you are feeling tense. Breathe in through your nose and out through your mouth. Relax your neck and shoulders to release stress. Work on your breathing for five minutes each day.
4. Think about your family members. How could you be more supportive of them? How could they be more supportive of you? Talk with your family about carrying out some of your ideas.

YOU ARE NOT ALONE

Dealing with family changes can make you feel hopeless and alone. But you are NOT alone. There are good people who care about you and want to help. There are also many resources you can use to learn more and help yourself.

Explore some of these ways to find the kindness and support you deserve.

People to Ask for Help

- ☑ guidance counselor
- ☑ teacher
- ☑ principal
- ☑ assistant principal
- ☑ parent
- ☑ older sibling
- ☑ grandparent
- ☑ aunt or uncle
- ☑ coach
- ☑ school secretary
- ☑ bus driver
- ☑ religious youth group leader
- ☑ any friend that you trust
- ☑ any adult that you trust

Websites

California Courts: Kids Guide to Separation and Divorce

www.familieschange.ca.gov/en/kids
Learn how to deal with separation and divorce in your family.

DoSomething.org: A Teenager's Guide to Dealing with Family Tension

dosomething.org/article/a-teenagers-guide-to-dealing-with-family-tension
Find tips and strategies for coping with family problems.

Nemours KidsHealth: Feelings

kidshealth.org/en/kids/feeling
Learn about different types of emotions and strategies for dealing with them.

Books

Baruch-Feldman, Caren, and Rebecca Comizio. *The Resilience Workbook for Kids: Fun CBT Activities to Help You Bounce Back from Stress and Grow from Challenges*. New Harbinger Publications, 2022.

O'Neill, Poppy. *I Can Handle Change: A Child's Guide to Facing New Challenges*. Sky Pony Press, 2023.

Stephenson, Catherine. *The Kids' Book of Family Changes: Understanding Divorce and Separation and Managing Feelings*. Wooden House Books, 2024.

Phone Helplines

Crisis Text Line

Text HOME to 741741 or message on WhatsApp. Young people of color can text STEVE to 741741 to reach culturally trained counselors.

LGBT National Youth Talkline

1-800-246-7743

National Suicide Prevention Lifeline

1-800-273-8255

Suicide and Crisis Lifeline

Call or text 988.

GLOSSARY

adapt (uh-DAPT)

To make changes in response to a new situation or challenge; to change

adrenaline (uh-DREN-uh-lin)

A hormone released in your body when you need more energy or when you sense danger

anxiety (ang-ZYE-i-tee)

Feelings of worry or fear

cope (kope)

To successfully deal with a problem or issue

cortisol (KOR-tuh-suhl)

A hormone produced when the body is under stress

depression (di-PRESH-uhn)

Unhappiness that doesn't go away

devastated (DEV-uh-stay-ted)

Extremely upset, especially by a major loss or disappointment

disoriented (dis-OR-ee-uhn-tid)

Feeling lost and confused

disruptions (dis-RUHP-shuhnz)

Disturbances or interruptions of ordinary activities

foundation (foun-DAY-shuhn)
The basis of something; the bottom level that supports a structure

isolate (EYE-suh-layt)
To stay away from other people

optimistic (ahp-tuh-MIS-tik)
Believing that things will turn out well; positive

overwhelmed (oh-vur-WELMD)
Overpowered by thoughts, feelings, and demands; having a strong emotional response to circumstances

predictable (pri-DIK-tuh-buhl)
Able to be known or seen in advance; in line with usual patterns or routines

resilient (ri-ZIL-yuhnt)
Able to recover from bad things that happen or adjust to changes; being strong during tough times

resist (ri-ZIST)
To refuse to accept; to fight back or struggle against

shock (shahk)
Feeling the effects of a sudden, unexpected, upsetting event

stress (stres)
Worry, strain, or pressure

validate (VAL-i-dayt)
To affirm or support the truth of something

INDEX

ABOUT THE AUTHOR

Kelli Hicks is a teacher, mom, and author who lives in Tampa, Florida. She has experienced many family changes in her life. She tries to remember that many changes are good and that she has lots of support to help her deal with tough challenges. Kelli makes sure to recognize and name her emotions to help her deal with the stress of family changes.